THE ISUIKWUATO NIGHT NURSE:
A BIOGRAPHY OF ROSELINE IHEDIWANMA OKONKWO, 1940-2024

AF131969

THE ISUIKWUATO NIGHT NURSE:
A BIOGRAPHY OF ROSELINE IHEDIWANMA OKONKWO, 1940-2024

Uche Uwaezuoke Okonkwo

GALDA VERLAG 2025

Bibliografische Information der Deutschen
Nationalbibliothek
Die Deutsche Nationalbibliothek verzeichnet diese
Publikation in der Deutschen
Nationalbibliografie; detaillierte bibliografische Daten
sind im Internet über
https://dnb.de abrufbar.

ISBN 978-3-96203-413-9 (Print)
ISBN 978-3-96203-414-6 (E-Book)

TABLE OF CONTENTS

ACKNOWLEDGEMENTS

Upon her exit in late October 2024, I reached out to various people, especially the people of Isuikwuato on my thinking of writing and publishing a biography in honour of my mother Roseline Ihediwanma Okonkwo. I thank Engr. Chukwunenye Umahi, Hon. Sunny Adimonyema, and Hon. Ogechi Omenka for providing tips on their aunt which enriched my source of writing, and of course, for my trip to Isuikwuato which enriched the manuscript.

The Librarians in the Department of History and International Studies at the University of Nigeria, Nsukka, helped me to source the materials needed to write this book, especially undergraduate thesis on Isuikwuato. I thank Glory Nwakanma and Dolapo, my former students, for their technical and intellectual assistance.

The staff of the National Archives Enugu, especially Maryjoe Oru, aided me with a lot of materials on Isuikwuato, and Daniel, my former student, was there to assist as well. At home, I received vital information from Jonathan Okonkwo, Chukwudi Anyiwo, James Anyiwo, and others. Okechi Ofoegbu is appreciated for long years of selfless service to my mum as our maternal relation. I am responsible for a few stylistic and chronological mistakes found in the book.

CHAPTER ONE

INTRODUCTION

Nursing as a profession began in 300 AD in the Roman Empire but became prominent in Europe during the Middle Ages with the profession expanding in scope in the 10th and 11th centuries.[1] Nurses during this period were not in the orbit of historical writing except for the event of the Crimean War of 1850 which brought Florence Nightingale to prominence as a nurse who devoted her strength to war victims as a social reformer and thus opened up a new vista for historians to write about nurses.[2] As a result, Florence Nightingale's book *Notes on Nursing* marked an important milestone in inculcating the contributions of nurses to historical traditions and scholarship.[3]

---

[1] Yolanda Smith, History of Nursing, http://news-medical.net accessed 16 October 2024

[2] Yolanda Smith, History of Nursing, cited

[3] History and Foundation-Nursing Fundamentals-pressbooks. pub, http://wtcs.pressbooks.pub accessed 2 November 2024

Globally, the history of famous nurses in Europe has been written. They include Florence Nightingale, Clara Barton, Claire Bertschinger, Florence Guinness Blake, Mary Breckinridge, Dorothea Dix, Mary Eliza Mahoney, Linda Richards, and Margaret Sander just to mention but few. In Nigeria, three nurses namely Kofoworola Abeni Pratt, Agholor Mary Ozuruonye, and Olubukola Mary Akinpelu have received cursory mention for their contribution to the nursing profession but no detailed biography of these great individuals has been taken up by historians.[4]

I am aware that an account of a prominent nurse Mary Slessor has been taken up by a scholar friend Professor David Imbua of the University of Calabar, Nigeria. His works eulogized Mary Slessor but ended up insisting that many achievements associated with her personality were done by her predecessors, especially on the issue of the killing of twins.[5] As a revisionist Historian, I insist that Imbua's paper does not eminently qualify as a biography of a hardworking nurse and a teacher like Mary Slessor. He was rather interested in

---

[4]   Top 3 Nurses in Nigerian History Who Made Significant Changes, http://dailytimesng.com accessed 3 November 2024

[5]   David Lishilinimle Imbua, 'Robbing Others to Pay Mary Slessor: Unearthing the Authentic Heroes and Heroines of the Abolition of Twin-Killing in Calabar, *African Economic History, Vol.41, 2013*, 139-158

addressing what he considered as a gap in Calabar and indeed Nigerian historiography.

Based on the above premise, there is a paucity of literature focusing on nurses and their contributions to nation-building. The reason for this intellectual misnomer is that Nigerian Historians are usually not eager to do biographical research except for a few developments that began in the last three decades.[6] Be that as it may, the earliest attempts to write about Africa by her own people at the professional level was dominated by political and economic historians especially to respond to the assertion of Eurocentric scholars led by Professor Trevor Roper during his inaugural lecture delivered at Oxford University in 1950 that Africa was darkness and that darkness was not a subject in History.[7] The African nationalist schools at Ibadan, Zaria, Dakar, Kenya, and Dar es Salaam were in a hurry to develop a nationalist school to debunk the assertion that Africa was like a yam tendril that needed to be directed to its stake. Apart from skeletal works on African kingdoms, empires, kings, and queens, there was less focus on carrying

---

[6] Winifred E. Akoda, *From the Abyss of Memory: Efiong Ukpong Aye, Calabar*, Desertwater Communications, 2011

[7] Nicodemus Fru Awasom & Ousman M. Bojang, 'Bifurcated World of African Nationalist Historiography" *Lagos Historical Review Vol.9*, 2009, 26

out biographical research by the first generation of African historians.

Regrettably, some of the earliest attempts towards biographical writings from professional historians primarily targeted key political and public figures.[8] Following this development, Professor Ademola Ajayi of the University of Ibadan in his 2023 inaugural lecture insists that biographical studies ought to be part of nation building project intended to inspire, to show what was accomplished and how to instill feelings of patriotism by encouraging readers to identify with the biography's subject.[9] This leads us to the question of asking, 'Who should be at the center stage of biography'? Is it the strong, wealthy, and the affluent? Where exactly is the history of those silent individuals who through hard work had made an impact in their respective societies? Probably, what is wrong with writing the history of middle-class people?

---

[8]   Nina E. Mba, *Ayoji Rosiji Man With Vision*, Ibadan, Spectrum Books, 1992; Phyllis Johnson, Eye of Fire Emeka Anyaoku, Ibadan, Spectrum Books, 2000 and Chijioke Ngobili, Ugwu Nwasike: The Man, The Name, The Monument: The Authored Biography of Warrant Chief Timothy Muodozie Nwasike of Ikenga-Ogidi 1879-1970, Lagos, Hillysyke Foundations, 2022

[9]   Simon Ademola Ajayi, Who is Not Afraid of History? Inaugural Lecture 2021/2022, University of Ibadan, Friday 6 July 2023, 38

Arising from these contests, this book focuses not on a political figure but a quiet selfless nurse, a wife, sister, mother, grandmother, and a very private person by every standard. Roseline Ihediwanma Okonkwo fits into these descriptions. Like every other works of biography, Night Nurse the title of this work was drawn from the song and album of a Jamaican reggae artiste Gregory Isaac released under the Tuff Gong Musical label in 1982. Part of the lyrics reads thus:

"Tell her your best, just to make it quick
Whom attended to the sick
Cause there must be something she can do
This heart is broken in two
Tell her it's a case of emergency
There's a patient by the name of Gregory
Night Nurse
Only you alone can quench this Jah thirst
My Night Nurse
Oh the pain is getting worse
I don't want to see no doc
I need attendance from my nurse around the clock"

Furthermore, Joyce Carol Oates excellent article "The Night Nurse" published in 1993 further gives credence to the plights of nurses working in the rural areas especially in night shifts.[10] Ladee Hubbard still on Night Nurses insists that even in darkness or fluorescent lights, the nurses worked in the absence of the medical doctors.[11] The virtues of Night Nurses as encapsulated in the works of Gregory Isaac, Joyce Carol Oates, Ladee Hubbard and Beatrice Murphy[12] exemplifies the attitude of Roseline to work in Oguta, Ejemekwuru, Ntezi, Effium, Oborrottu (now Opuoma), Ohaozara, Ndoro Umuahia and every other place she worked. Roseline Okonkwo was one devoted Nurse whose sense of duty, diligence, hard work, spirituality and humane life deserves academic documentation and hence this book.

Roseline Ihediwanma Okonkwo was one of the foot soldiers of Professor Olukoya Ransome Kuti's Primary Health Care (PHC) vision. Kuti as the Minister for Health, was instrumental towards the launching of the National Health Policy

---

[10] Joyce Carol Oates, 'The Night Nurse', *Ploughwares Vol.19 No.4 Borderlands (Winter 1993/1994)*, 104-120

[11] Ladee Hubbard, The Night Nurses, *Callalo*, Vol.39, No.4, 2016, 775-778

[12] Beatrice Murphy, Diary of A Night Nurse, Butte, Montana, 1909, *Montana The Magazine of Western History, Vol.39 No.4, Autumn 1989*, 64-70

in 1988[13]. The PHC as established was a major health care revolution policy created by a globally respected medical expert and scholar of all times. The philosophy behind this major health policy has been jettisoned since the return of democratic rule in Nigeria in 1999 and this has further exacerbated problems leading to an increase in mortality rates since the primary health care and general hospitals are all gone thus leaving the rural chemist and tertiary hospitals like Federal Medical centers, Teaching and Specialist hospitals to bear the brunt of every health challenges emanating mostly from the rural areas.

---

[13]   Nwankwo, Chinyere I, 'International Organizations and the Development of Primary Health care in Nigeria, 1988-2009, *BA Project, Department of History, UNN* April, 2009, 44

CHAPTER TWO

BACKGROUND AND GROWTH

She was born on 10 October 1940 to Mr. and Mrs. Pepple and Kezaih Ogbusue Omenka of Umuihe village Eluama Isuikwuato now in Abia State, Nigeria as Roseline Ihediwanma Ogbusue Omenka. Roseline's father got the name Pepple from Bonny where he served as a cook.[14]

Her place of birth Isuikwuato could be described as hilly country formerly of the Okigwe Division but now Isuikwuato Local Government Area of Abia State, Nigeria.[15] As a large town, Isuikwuato consists of sixteen villages namely Ahaba, Ezere, Ovim, Isiyi, Amuta, Eluama, Amibo, Amiyi, Umunnekwu, Nunya, Acha and Umuasuaa.[16] It was categorized as one of the six clans in the Okigwe area with others

---

[14] Burial Programme of Rev. Omenka O. Omenka at Wesley Methodist Church Cathedral Eluama, Isuikwuato, 28-07-2018

[15] L.O Ndukwe, Isuikwuato: "A Pre Colonial Economy" *BA Project, Department of History, UNN April*,1995, 4

[16] Ndukwe, Isuikwuato: "A Pre Colonial Economy" 4

including Otanchara, Otanzu, Isuochi, Nneato and Umuchieze.[17] Isuikwuato lies between longtitude 7^0 23 E and latitude $5^{0.4N}$ and 5.5^N.[18]

Source: JOFAM Files, Mrs Kezaih Omenka (Roseline's Mother)

[17]   Mazi C.O Udeagha, 'Trade and Trade Routes Within The Okigwe Area in the 19th Century" *TransAfrican Journal of History, Vol.16,* 1987, 78

[18]   Ekekwe James Obinna, A History of the Apostolic Faith Church of Jesus Christ in Amaba Isuikwuato (1941-1960), B.A Project in History and International Studies University of Nigeria, October 2007, 8

The Intelligence Report on Isuikwuato as of 1933 captured in Onyenkpa's thesis estimated that they had a population of 27,000 with a land mass of 144 square kilometers. The 1952/53 census places the people as numbering 22,225 males and 25,887 females was estimated population of 48, 806 but a decrease was recorded in the 1963 census to a figure of about 43,313.[19] The 2006 population census places Isuikwuato to a population of about 115, 794.[20]

Geographically, Isuikwuato is bounded by the east by Alayi and Uzuakoli in the Bende Local Government Area; in the west by Otanchara and Otanzu clans of the Okigwe Local Government Area; in the north by Uturu and Ishiagu in Okigwe and Afikpo respectively and in the south by Ohuhu in Ikwuano/Umuahia Local Government Area.[21] Isuikwuato is also bound by Alayi and Ugwueke in the south, Akolo, Mkpa and Amoji in the east and as well as Uturu, Okigwe and Ihube in the north.[22]

---

[19] Chijioke Onyebuchi Onyenkpa, "A Historical Survey of Isuikwuato Before 1900: Origins, Pattern of Migration and Settlement and Political Organization", *BA Project History and Archaeology*, University of Nigeria, Nsukka, 1981,1

[20] Isuikwuato Local Government Area of Nigeria, http://www.city population accessed 12 November,2024

[21] Ogbuagu Adibe Chukwuma, "Warfare in Pre-colonial Isuikwuato" *BA Project Department of History,* University of Nigeria,Nsukka, June, 1989,4

[22] Umejiaku Vera Uche, 'Local Government and Community

Isuikwuato's tradition of origin like any other pre-literate Igbo society is difficult to reconstruct. However, available records indicates that Obiangwu was the progenitor of the people. The first son of Obiangwu was Enyi. Enyi had 3 wives who gave birth to three children that formed the Isuikwuato clan. The children of Enyi's first wife gave birth to Ahaba (Senior town of the clan) Ovim and Ezere. The second wife gave birth of Isiyi, Amaba, Umuasua, Umuobiala, Eluama, Amuta, Otampa, Amebe and the third wife gave birth to Amaibo, Amiyi, Atcha, Umunekwu and Nunya. These three groups of towns are known as Ime-Enyi or Ahaba (The Senior Group), and Ogudu-asa or Amaibo (the third group).[23]

A detailed analysis of the Isuikwuato people further asserts that Obiangwu was an itinerant trader who had three wives. The first wife gave birth to the first son Enyi, the second wife gave birth to the second son Awu, while the third son gave birth to Ogudu and these three brothers settled in Ahaba until population pressure set in. According to the report, the descendants of

---

Development in Isuikwuato LGA 1976-2000, *BA Project History and International Studies,* University of Nigeria, Nsukka, 2019, 9

[23]   NAE (Hereafter National Archives Enugu), CSE 1/85/4132, File No EP 7576 A, Intelligence Report on Isu Ikwu Ato clan by Mr V.Fox Strangeways, District Officer Okigwe, 1930-1933

Enyi were known as Imenyi which consists of Ahaba, Ovim, and Ezere. They are known as Isuamawu. Isuamawu comprised of Isiyi, Amaba, Umuobila, Eluama, Amuda, Otampa, Amuta, Umuasua and Amebe which was later absorbed by Umuobila. The descendants of Ogudu are known as Oguduasa meaning seven groups or sons. These group of villages include Amaibo, Amiyi, Acha, Umunnekwu, and Nnunya., The other group are the Ahmadu and Amasiri. The Amadu was later absorbed by Acha village group due to their small population while the Amaisisi group also settled with the people of Oguduasaa.[24]

In his account of the Ahaba people in Isuikwuato, Eke-Aghukwa traced the origin of the people and attempted providing nearly possible dating that Okaraka was the founder who was older than Obiangwu (1583-1613); Enyi (1613-1643); Aba (1643-1673); Iyi (1673-1733), Osiawa (1733-1763); Unknown (1733-1767), Ikere Ukwu (1763-1793); Ikere Nta (1793-1823); Ndukwe (1823-1853); Oku (1853-1883) and Ndukwe Oku (1883-19..).[25]

---

[24]   Ogbuagu Adibe Chukwuma, "Warfare in Pre-colonial Isuikwuato" 5

[25]   Ihuoma Ngozi Eke-Aghukwa, A Historical Survey of Ahaa (Ahaba) in Isuikwuato Local Government Area Before the 1900, BA Project in History, June 1983, 10-11

Isuikwuato according to Umejiaku is symbolic and literally signifies three clans namely Imenyi, Oguduasaa and Isuamawu.[26] An account of Isuikwuato was given as three brothers who are all of Isu stock.[27] Over the years, scholars have made attempt to examine Isu migration theory in Igbo history. One of such scholar is valentine Alakwe who insists that Isu people are traders and hawkers who originally have no fixed home. He affirms that the second son of Enyi in Isuikwuato had Amaibo, Acha, Umunnekwu and Nunya who are of the Isu migration stock. For this famous archivists, Isu migrations is associated with Igbo towns originally from Amaigbo-Isu-Orlu/Nkwerre axis with the affix of Isu attached to their names. According to him, such towns include Isu Njaba, Isu Ofe iyi, Isuikwuato and Isu ofia.[28] AFigbo a renowned Igbo Historian opines that Isuama Igbo simply implies the Igbo who had gone abroad and are made up of Mbawa, Mbieri, Ikeduru, Osu, Ehime, Ugboma, Mbaise, Ohuhu Ngwa and many Cross River Igbo group.[29]

---

[26] Umejiaku Vera Uche, "'Local Government and Community Development in Isuikwuato LGA 1976-2000", 9-10

[27] NAE,File No EP 7576^A CSE 1/85/4132, Intelligence Report on Isu Ikwu Ato

[28] Valentime A Alakwe, *The History of Nkwerre-Isu Igbo*, Glasboro, Goldline and Jacobs Publishing, 2020, 41-60

[29] Adiele Afigbo, *Ropes of Sand: Studies in Igbo History and*

W.B Baikie an European explorer in 1854 identified Isuama Igbo speaking people as contracted form of Isu.[30] Following the 1841 Civilizing Mission to the Niger by the Church Missionary Society (CMS), Isuama spoken languages was identified in Sierra Leone as prominent Igbo dialect and was considered as a well spoken language for the Igbo Bible translation exercise.[31] Professor Isichei writing in 1976 identified Isuama as people who hired themselves as carriers to the oil producers in the Orata country and have transported produce to markets in New Calabar, River or Okirika.[32] The emphasis here is that Isuikwuato is a home of people who had migrated to their present place of abode at one time or the other. Onyenkpa postulation is that Isuikwuato would have been in their present place of abode around the 16th century.[33] This period to a

Culture, Ibadan, University Press Ltd, 1981, 12-13

[30] William Balfour Baikie, Narrative of An Exploring Voyage Up to the Rivers Kwora and Binue Commonly Known as the Niger and Tsadda in 1854, London, Frank Cass and Co Ltd, 1966, 300

[31] Uche Uwaezuoke Okonkwo, 'Archdeacon Dennis Union Igbo Through the Prisms of History" in Uche Uwaezuoke Okonkwo and Chijioke Chinoyerem Ekebuisi ed. *ACentenary of Archdeacon Dennis Union Igbo*, Uturu, Gregory University Press, 2018, 17

[32] Elizabeth Isichei, *Igbo Worlds: An Anthology of Oral Histories and Historical Descriptions*, London and Basingstoke, Macmillan, 1977, 279-280

[33] Onyenkpa, "A Historical Survey of Isuikwuato Before 1900:

large extent confirms with the Isu migration era in Igbo history. However, there is need to go beyond hypothesis and dig deep into more historical accounts that will validate these claims.

The background of Isuikwuato provided in this book is relevant in addressing basic misconceptions and misrepresentation of Isuikwuato people in doctored history. For example, V. Fox Strangeways an European District Officer in charge of Okigwe (1930-1933) had this to say about Isuikwuato people:

> The Isu-kwu-ato is a small clan of the Ibo tribe, inhabiting the eastern part of the Okigwe Division of the Owerri Province. They are extremely independent, suspicious and quickly tampered race, fond of intrigue and grasping. On the other hand they have undoubted intelligence, and a keen sense of humour, in fact, in these two respects they appear to surpass the other inhabitants of the division. Their shyness with strangers is accounted for

Origins, Pattern of Migration and Settlement and Political Organization" 16 by the nature of their country, which makes the establishment of proper communication a matter of extreme difficulty; while (paradoxical as it may seem) their intelligence and independence have no doubt been fostered by the labour and trade conditions which attended, and have followed the construction of the Nigerian Eastern Railways (sic).

He continued;

They have a keen class consciousness, but in spite of this or possibly because of it, for until recently they were split up between the Bende and Okigwi divisions-they have been somewhat difficult to administer, and have for at least the last ten years been regarded as the 'unruly children' of Bende and Okigwe divisions. Yet there is something like very likeable about the Isi-ikwu-ato; for beneath their rather surly exterior they are

> humorous and reasonable; and
> their vociferous stubbornness
> is perhaps preferable to the
> facile but meaningless docility
> characteristic of certain other
> clans (sic).[34]

This study on Roseline Okonkwo born during the colonial era in Isuikwuato repudiates the generalized false claims made by European imperialists. This book provides intellectual nuances and epistemological rearmament very relevant in advancing knowledge on colonial and post-colonial people in Africa. The assertion that Isuikwuato people are quick tempered, shy, difficult to administer and stubborn is not true. This is because the Isuikwuato people generally do not possess Strangeway's description. Achebe had postulated that until the lions produce their own historians, the story of hunt will continue to glorify the hunter and this is relevant at this point.[35] V. Vox Strangeways statement was made out of hatred and racial prejudice associated with British colonial rule. His Eurocentric perception of Isuikwuato is that of inferior races usually mooted

---

[34]   CSE 1/85/4132, File No EP 7576 A, Intelligence Report on Isu Ikwu Ato clan by Mr V.Fox Strangeways, cited

[35]   See Chinua Achebe, *Home and Exile*, London, Penguin Publishing Group, 2001

in imperial philosophy geared towards advancing social Darwinism ideologies. Social Darwinism had its root in Charles Darwin theory of evolution were he made derogatory remarks on inferior genes.

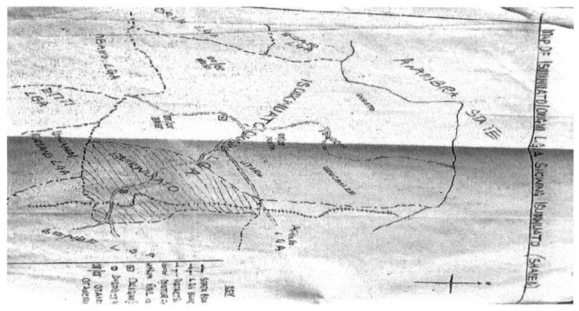

Source: See Chijioke Onyebuchi Onyenkpa, "A Historical Survey of Isuikwuato Before1900: Origins, Pattern of Migration and Settlement and Political Organization", *BA Project History and Archaeology*, University of Nigeria, Nsukka, 1981,1

ISUIKWUATO UNDER COLONIAL RULE & THE OMENKA FAMILY GROUP

Prior to 1929, the Isuikwuato clan was divided between the Bende and Okigwi Divisions. The Bende Division administred the Ahaba group comprising of Ahaba, Ovim and Nzere. They also administered Isiyi, Amaba, Umuasua, Otampa, and Amuta of Isu Ama awa group. The rest was under

Okigwi Division with clan court members who sat with the elders of the land Ndi Awa Ala.[36] The Clan Courts in Isuikwuato was divided into the following groups:

> Imenyi Group: Ahaba, Ovim and Ezere Isu-Ama-Awu: Isiyi, Amaba, Umuasua, Umuobiala, Eluama, Amuta and Otampa and Ogudu Asa Group: Amibo, Amiyi, Atcha, Umuneku and Nonya.[37]

The Isuikwuato Clan Council was set up in 1933 and by December 1936, the Council was firmly established.[38] The colonial regime in Isuikwuato was interested in raising revenue through tax collection from the people. In tax-related matters, a habit of forgoing the signatures of elders of the clan to protest exorbitant taxes was dictated by the colonial authorities.[39] The revenue derived from taxing local people was part of British colonial statecraft and

---

[36] NAE, OKDIST 9/1/241B, Proposals for the Future Administrative and Judicial Organization of Isu-ikwu-Ato Clan

[37] NAE, OKDIST 9/1/159,Report of Council Reorganization in Isuikwuato Clan

[38] NAE, OKDIST 9/1/109, ETC Ennals the Assistant District Officer Okigwi 'Report on Council Reorganization in Isuikwuato Clan

[39] NAE, OKDIST 9/1/106, Elders and Ezealas of Isuikwuato: Petition From

political economy. Just in 1938, about £8,487 from about 28,861 taxable adults from the Isuikwuato clan tax.[40] From this period to 1953 taxes was impose and collected from the people and yet it was only in 1953 that Nonya-Eluama road was cleared and widened by the colonial regime.[41] This further elucidates the fact that there were infrastructural injustices targeted at the colonized people not excluding Roseline's parents.

The creation of Native Courts in colonial Isuikwuato was not for the purpose of administering the area but strictly for revenue generation. In 1938, the newly elected Isuikwuato Clan Council began to sit.[42] The Isuikwuato clan was divided into 77 kindreds. The Amala-Ala (Compound Heads) and elders such as the Okeneme and Nde-Nkpa and youths were all committed in raising tax for the colonial regime.[43] Despite these arrangements, it was observed that in Isuamawu and Oguduasa, the problem of tax collection was that former tax

---

[40]   NAE, OKDIST 9/1/241B, Isuikwuato Clan Tax

[41]   NAE, OKDIST 6/1/54, A Letter from the Central Office Native Administration to the Native Authority Isuikwuato 'Nonya-Eluama Road'15 June 1953

[42]   NAE, OKDIST 9/1/159, A Letter from the District Officer Okigwe to the Resident Owerri Province Portharcourt Ísuikwuato Clan' 27 October 1938

[43]   NAE, OKDIST 9/1/159, Report on Council Re-Organization in Isuikwuato Clan

collectors were automatically court members.[44] Tax was so important to the colonial regime that one Ujombu Akamadu the Eze Ala of Umunekwu was in 1932 imprisoned for collecting taxes from 1929-1931 and remitted the same to the government without remitting the 1931 arrears of tax.[45] The colonial government was quick to appoint one Mr Agu of Amibo yet from another village group to collect taxes in Umunekwu despite oppositions against his appointment by the people.[46] A. E. Afigbo's in his article titled *The Native Treasury Question under the Warrant Chief System in Eastern Nigeria 1899-1929*, affirms that the Native Treasury was introduced by the High Commissioner of Southern Nigeria, Ralph Moor as source of revenue generation in colonial Eastern Nigeria. Under this oppressive tax regime, Roseline parents lived.[47]

---

[44]   NAE, OKDIST 9/1/159, Report on Council Re-Organization in Isuikwuato Clan

[45]   NAE, OKDIST 4/14/28, A Letter from Ujombu Akamadu to the District Office Okigwi, 14 June 1932

[46]   NAE, OKDIST 4/14/28, A Letter from Chief Ejeafor of Amibo to the Worship District Officer Okigwe, 27 August 1932

[47]   Adiele.E. Afigbo, "The Native Treasury Question under the Warrant Chief System in Eastern Nigeria 1899-1929", *University of Ife Journal of African Studies* 4, no.1, (1967): 30-32.

ROSELINE'S PARENTS & FAMILY CHART IN UMUIHE, ELUAMA ISUIKWUATO

PEPPLE OGBUSUE OMENKA & KEZAIH OMENKA
(CIRCA 1900 & 1908)

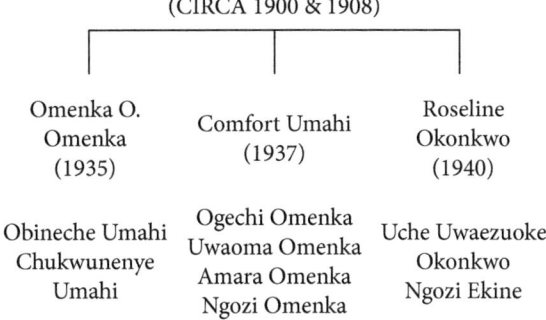

Omenka O. Omenka (1935)	Comfort Umahi (1937)	Roseline Okonkwo (1940)
Obineche Umahi Chukwunenye Umahi	Ogechi Omenka Uwaoma Omenka Amara Omenka Ngozi Omenka	Uche Uwaezuoke Okonkwo Ngozi Ekine

Roseline also called Nwanne was the third and the last child of the Omenka family arrived to the family in 1940. Her other siblings include Rev. Omenka Ogbusue Omenka, a former school principal and clergy of the Methodist Church, Nigeria. The second daughter of this family was Mrs. Comfort Umahi whom Roseline called 'Sister'. Suffice to say that Roseline's bond with the late sister Comfort is beyond the imagination of the present writer. They were fond of each other as Comfort's exist in 1999 affected Roseline in so many ways. Indeed, four defining moments affected Rose as a person. First was in 1979 when Obineche her nephew (Comfort's first son) passed on, second was death of his husband Jeremaih Okonkwo in 1998, the death of her sister Comfort in 1999 and Rev Omenka O. Omenka demise in 2018.

JOFAM Files, Pictiure of Omenka O. Omenka and Ogbuagu M.I Umeh during Roseline's and Jerry Okonkwo weeding in 1978

Omenka was highly respected by her two sisters and other relatives. As a student of the prestigious University of Nigeria, Nsukka in the late 1960s, Roseline and Comfort were always joyful carrying their brothers traveling box by foot from Eluama to Ovim a distance of about 6 kilometers which was then the nearest motor park from Isuikwuato to Enugu to enable him to get to the new University at Nsukka. Omenka fondly called Isaac by the mother who was known as "Brother" by the large family of the Umuihe clan in Eluama.

Omenka O. Omenka obtained B.Sc. degree in Physics with Bias in Mathematics from the University of Nigeria where he was enrolled as a student in 1966. His studies were interrupted by the Nigeria-Biafran War which lasted between 1967-1970 thus graduating in 1971 at the end of the bloody civil war. Omenka had during the war enlisted as a Biafran scientist working with the Research and Production (RAP) Unit of the defunct republic. This unit was responsible for indigenous-made rockets and bombs (ogbunigwe as the most popular among them), repairs, maintenance, and manufacturing even during the threats of war.

During the war years, Roseline returned to Eluama her place of birth. Eluama was pretty save said Roseline but the hardship that was ubiquitous in Biafra was also felt by the people. The federal troops arrived Isuikwuato on 28 March 1968 at Amoke Amiyi and Umunnekwu villages. The encounter between the Federal troops and the Biafran soldiers were fierce that many deaths were recorded in Akara-Ahaba axis.[48] The war ended on 12 January 1970 and Roseline returned to Abakaliki as we shall be examining later in this book. The Civil war which affected and still affect many Igbo homes was unnecessary and was a class struggle among the rank and file in the Nigerian army. Ojukwu had rejected Gowon's emergence as the new leader after the July Counter Coup of 1966 because Brigadier Ogundipe the most senior military officer was supposed to assume the position of Head of State after General Aguiyi Ironsi who got to power following Nzeogwu's coup of January 1966. Could Ojukwu have become Military Governor of the Eastern region as it were when the likes of Brigadiers Alexander Madiebo, Hilary Njoku, and others from the same region were his seniors in the army? Arthur Nwankwo in his book *The Challenge of Biafra* noted that there were no arms, all firearms including Dane guns were commandeered and the rest were armed with machetes, clothed, and moved to the forest to face

---

[48]   Nwosu Joseph Ihedinihu, The Nigerian Civil War and Isuikwuato Women, *BA Project in History, University of Nigeria, Nsukka*, April 1995, 25-27

a force armed with machine guns and automatic rifles [49] How else could Col. Ojukwu's insensitivity be described as a trained soldier who had boasted that no power in Africa could subdue Biafra and he had no firearms? How could our properly trained Military Officers that were in charge in Biafra allow our youths (about 10,000) drawn from many places in Igboland to Nsukka in 1967 to use cutlass to face well-equipped federal troops with machine guns in the name of defending Biafra in the Opi/Nsukka axis of the war in 1967? For the present writer, young people were lured to commit suicide. Who were the 335 elders upon whose resolution Biafra was declared?

This is important here following the rise of Unknown Gunmen (UG) and the invasion of several Igbo villages by the military in 2021. These villages include Egbuoma where Roseline lived as a retired nurse. She had seen threats of civilian populace, attacks, and death that took place in 1967 raising its ugly head again. Future historians will have difficulties in understanding and interpreting the effects and loss of lives of both agitators and state security men in the Orlu and Okigwe axis of Imo State Nigeria since 2021. The history and politics of memory will engage such scholars.

---

[49]   Arthur A. Nwankwo, Nigeria: The Challenge of Biafra, Enugu, Fourth Dimension, 1972, 16

Rev. Omenka's marriage to Mrs. Bridget Omenka (also a retired Principal of the school) was also a success story of an ideal Igbo family. Omenka's teaching career blossomed during his long stay at Trinity High School Oguta. His home in Oguta became a haven of sorts for relations of his who had their education in Oguta.

JOFAM Files, This is the picture of Mrs. Bridget Omenka with Ogechi and Uwaoma

Blessed by two prominent schools Priscilla Memorial Grammar School (PMGS) and Trinity High School founded by Sir Richard Nzimiro and Sir Philip Udom. Omenka had blissful career with Bridget until he moved to Aba and retired as a school principal to become a 'Fisher of Men' in the Methodist Church, Nigeria in 1988 after successful bagging a Diploma in Theology from the Methodist Theological Institute, Umuahia.

JOFAM Files, This is the picture of the ordination of Rev Omenka O. Omenka in 1989. The Pictures contain Isuikwuato family members Mrs Comfort Umahi, Bridget Omenka, Sunny Adimonyema, Mgborie Adimonyenma, Uche Okonkwo, Ndubuisi Adimonyema, Ngozi Okonkwo, Kate (late), Amara Omenka, Ogechi Omenka, and others

CHAPTER THREE

EDUCATION, CAREER DEVELOPMENT AND FAMILY LIFE

Roseline went to school at a time when it was difficult for the education of the Girl Child (GC). Following the arrival of the European Methodist Missionary in 1915 to Isuikwuato, the history of Western education began in the area. This was marked by the arrival of Rev. R. Cawthrone to Ovim.[50]

In Eluama, Roseline's place of birth, the first primary school was established in Umuebele in October 1916.[51] The Isu Central School situated between Amiyi and Eluama was established in 1929.[52] Still in 1936, there was petition to the Native

---

[50] Okoronkwo O. Kingdom, Christianity and Western Education in Isuikwuato 1906-1994, *BA Project, Department of History,* University of Nigeria, Nsukka, April 1995, 18
[51] Okoronkwo, Christianity and Western Education in Isuikwuato 1906-1994, 19
[52] Okoronkwo, Christianity and Western Education in Isuikwuato 1906-1994, 20

Adminstration in Isuikwuato demanding that schools should be built. A capital expenditure of £200 was budgeted for erecting schools and about 4 youths were sent to the Uyo Teaching Trainning School to qualify as teachers.[53] As of 1936, there was only two Native Administration Schools situated in Isuochi and one in the Isu area.[54] In 1937, the Isuikwuato clan requested the establishment of Middle 111 and Middle IV schools. At this period, Capt. Leeming of Okigwi Division replied that Isuikwuato cannot afford such schools but he directed that the Native Administration should build similar schools like the ones in Ngodo and Amucha Division.[55]

During this period, as available records reveals, there was no room for girls education since they girls as it was believed needed no education except for the informal.[56] Roseline had acquired basic informal education in cooking, basketry (nkata), farming, pottery, local soap and candle

---

[53]   NAE, OKDIST 9/1/126, A Memorandum from the District Officer Okigwe Division to the Resident Owerri Province Portharcourt, 10 October 1936

[54]   NAE, OKDIST 9/1/126, A Memorandum from the District Officer Okigwe Division to the Resident Owerri Province Portharcourt 'Ebi and Others, 10 October 1936

[55]   NAE, OKDIST 9/1/126, A Memorandum from the District Officer Okigwe Division to the Resident Owerri Province Portharcourt 'Ebi and Others, 26 January 1937

[56]   Okoronkwo, 20

(egbenduru made from palm oil shaft). As a girl from an average family, farming sustained the family especially the availability of various markets such as Ahonta, Nkwo Ukwu, Nkwonta, Eke-Ukwu, Eke nta, Aho-Ukwu and Orie nta markets. The eze-iyi and Adaoma was a daily routine in the family as the only source of water in the absence of rain water. Mbonu Francis Onyebuchi reveals that each isuikwuato market have a market attended by people far and near. These markets include Nkwo Nnunya, Eke Umuokogbue, Afonta Eluama, Nkwo Amaba, Orie Ahaba, Oriendu Ovim, Aho Acha, Eke Amiyi, Eke Obilohia, Aho Amaibo, Eke Ozara, Eke Umuobiala, Orie Otampa, Nkwonta Umunekwu and Orienta Umunekwu Agbo.[57]

Still, in education, the schools established in Isukwuato had their problems. For example, by 1945, none of the schools in Ahaba, Ovim, and Eluama could afford to offer admission to pupils in Upper Classes. It was not until 1951 that the Methodist Schools at Ovim and Eluama were approved by the Ministry of Education to prepare for the First School Leaving Certificate Examination (FLSC).[58]

---

[57]   Mbonye, Francis Onyebuchi, 'External Trade of Isuikwuato in the Nineteenth Century" BA Project, Department of History, University of Nigeria, Nsukka, June 1987, 15

[58]   Okoronkwo, 23-24

Name of School	Grade	Number of Classes	Number of Teachers	Number of Pupils	Boys	Girls
Nunya	JP	3	2	82	46	36
Amaibo	SP	6	5	178	105	73
Amaba-Umuasua	SP	9	9	319	166	153
Ahaba	SP	18	19	598	307	291
Spencer Girls Ovim	SP	07	07	261	-----	261
Oguduasa Central	SP	06	06	209	131	78
Ovim	SP	11	12	390	357	33
Eluama	SP	12	12	431	245	186
Otampa	SP	09	08	237	151	136

Source: Okoronkwo O. Kingdom, Christianity and Western Education in Isuikwuato 1906-1994, *BA Project, Department of History,* University of Nigeria, Nsukka, April 1995, 24

Roseline attended Eluama Methodist Central School Isuikwuato and passed the First School Leaving Certificate (FLSC) conducted on 25 November 1960.

From 1960-1962, she attended secondary school in Ikot Ekpene and Emmanuel College Owerri. Following economic difficulties, she moved to secure job in April 1962 as a ward maid in Ishielu in Abakaliki Division. She was later trained as a nurse at Oji River School of Nursing.

Source: JOFAM Files, Roseline Okonkwo receiving her certificate from the Rector at the end of her programme at the School of Nursing Oji River

Source: JOFAM Files, Roseline Okonkwo at the School of Nursing Choral Society with other colleagues at the School of Health Technology, Oji River

Her appointment as Ward Maid did not affect her dream of acquiring education. Much later in 1974, she sat and passed private GCE examination.

Source: JOFAM Files, Roseline Okonkwo at the School of Nursin with other colleagues at the School of Health Technology, Oji River

Roseline Ihediwanma Ogbusue as a Nurse in 1962 (Third person from the left)

She attended the School of Health Technology Aba from 13th January 1976 - 30th June 1977 and successfully completed a course for Rural Health Assistants. From September 1981 to August 1982, Ihediwanma obtained a Certificate for Community Health Assistants at the School of Health Technology in Aba. In June 1983, the Federal Ministry of Health certified her as a Community Assistant. Between 1988 to 1990, Roseline bagged Diploma in Community Health Supervisor at the School of Health Technology, Aba.

Source: JOFAM Files, Roseline as an athlete in the Nursing School

Between 1988 to 1990, Roseline lived with Uche and Ngozi her children in the Omenka family apartment at Ovom Girls Secondary School were Mrs. Bridget Omenka was teaching at the time. There was rules when to eat, rest, work, play football and compulsory reading. Mrs. Bridget will issue us new books like Flora Nwapa *Efuru* and *Idu*, Achebe's *Man of the People and Things Fall Apart*, Nkem Nwankwo's *My Mercedes is Bigger than Yours* and Cyprian Ekwensi's *Jagua Nana*. We all read these books compulsorily as primary school pupils. Mrs Omenka was tough and students feared her for stand on discipline. There was the stubborn Ihuoma Nwagba who was handed over to Mrs. Bridget at the time.

Roseline who was in Nursing School will always wake in the morning to refer to Rev Omenka as Brother. Rev Omenka took care of everyone, prayers were compulsory and football was not played on Sundays because it was a Sabbath day that must be kept holy. Roseline believed in her brother and sister so much. For, example, it was Rev. Omenka who took me to All Saints Secondary School Ehere after I concluded Primary School at Ehere Ogbor Community Primary School Aba in 1990 to register me as a student. Our best days were Saturdays as Auntie Juan, Amauche and Kate were in charge of cooking delicious beans, while Ogechi, Uwaoma, Amara, and myself were responsible for fetching water. Water was indeed a scarce commodity in Aba during this period.

CAREER AND RETIREMENT

Roseline started her carrier as a Ward Maid on 1st April 1962 on a salary scale of £62.0.0s.0d monthly at Ishielu County Council.[59] Following the various government civil service reforms her salary increased. For example, the Morgan Civil Service reform with effect from 1 April 1964 placed her on a salary scale of £78.05.0s.0d monthly.[60] At the end of the Nigeria-Biafra War From the 1st of April 1972, Adebo commission made her earn £166.05.0s.0d monthly.[61] The Udoji award of 1974 made her earned N830 as a Clinical Assistant.[62] On 1st June 1977, she was elevated to the position of Rural Health Assistant and on 1st September 1982, she became Community Health Assistant while on 1st May 1987 she was made Community Health Supervisor and of 1st May 1997 she was elevated to Chief Health Assistant and her retirement came 1st April 1997.[63]

---

[59]   JOFAM Files, Mgborokwu D.M ''Salary Progression in Respect of Mrs R.I Okonkwo
[60]   JOFAM Files, Records of Service (Cond) Africansta
[61]   JOFAM Files, Mgborokwu D.M ''Salary Progression in Respect of Mrs R.I Okonkwo
[62]   JOFAM Files, Mgborokwu D.M ''Salary Progression in Respect of Mrs R.I Okonkwo
[63]   JOFAM Files, Mgborokwu D.M ''Salary Progression in Respect of Mrs R.I Okonkwo

The salary scale placed on Roseline by the government was not without excessive tax demand of compulsory income tax.[64] Regrettably, the attitude of the government in subsequent years of Roseline retirement especially in paying monthly pension commensurate with her taxes while at work remains just an enigma. Between 1977 and 1983, she worked in the Health Centre at Oguta. The focus of the Primary Health Care (PHC) was to diagnose, treat and provide vital health information to the community. They were in charge of vaccinating against yellow fever, polio, tuberculosis, and other communicable diseases. The center at Oguta handles other health challenges and usually makes referrals of complicated cases to the Oguta General Hospital. From 1983-1985, she worked at the Health Center Dispensary in Ejemekwuru. She had just arrived in the community and the previous occupant of the government quarters was finding it difficult to quit. After leaving the place, he continued to embarrass Roseline and even made life-threatening attempts. The Ejemekwuru people stood by Roseline and it was later found that there was frauds in accounting for government funds. Roseline was not only diligent but humble. She nearly got into trouble in Ejemekwuru in the case

---

[64]   JOFAM Files, Income Tax P.A.Y.E Receipt, 1976-1997

of a man who usually begs for alms and visits the health center. Roseline had just returned to Obudi Agwa on a fateful day when the man came around as usual. Obudi Agwa as of this period was known for garri production and a species of yam known as *Ji nwe so so* which my mum cherishes a lot. She had just given the man garden egg which she shared with everyone of us in the house. We lived with sister Onyenaturuchi Adimonyenma and we all ate the garden egg. While still cooking in the kitchen, the man who usually sits in the corridor has just died. The case would have been different if not for Roseline's kind of character. The man was buried after all, but I was surprised to see that the man had relations who were able to afford money to buy beer for people to drink during the funeral.

In Oborottu (now Opuoma), Roseline worked between 1985-1987. Our Landlord was one Chief Nwokocha whose house was next to Chief Nwagiriga. Chief Nwagiriga's kids Gift and Adaeze were our playmates. Chief Nwokocha was a core traditionalist and had a polygamous home. He had a son Nwalor and the second wife had a daughter who was in constant disagreement with the father. It was from Chief Nwokocha's mouth that I first heard about the Igbo word *Tufiakwa*. He usually said that to the daughter each time he gets pissed off. Roseline developed strong bond with the people of the area that during the Omerife festivals we usually got gifts from the people of the community. There was a well built hospital in Oborottu built by the oil firm operating in the area. Roseline was indeed a night nurse moving out at night to ensure safe delivery of pregnant women in the area. She would also return early in the morning to attend to her compulsory early morning prayers. God was gracious to us in Opuoma. Onyenaturuchi had left after her primary school in Oborottu and there was Ngozi Emenike who lived with us. It was one sacred day that swimming in the Urashi river was not encouraged. It was advised that people who must swim must not make noise as they will be disturbing the water goddess. Ngozi Emenike who just arrived from Isuikwuato would not hear. As she attempted to swim with other indigenes, she didn't want to believe that local people of the area hardly drown in the river. It took the intervention of Mrs. Nwagiriga the mother of Gift who rescued Ngozi and I heard her thank the water spirit for not failing her. This is one incident that stopped us from going to the river but in later years it shaped my research prospects of working and researching about the water spirits in Igbo spirituality.

From 1987-1988, Roseline was posted back to Oguta and we have left Oborottu for good. She continued to work diligently and extended bonds of friendship at home and work place. We returned to the same building Number 6 Eneke road and this time, we had Mr. Francis Anyaeji of Okichi village as our neighbor. Francis Anyaeji had a red Volkswagen beatles which he drove from Monday to Friday to Owerri where he worked. The wife Adeline from Umudanike village Oguta was a workaholic catereer. Her children include Uche whom will refer to as Uche nwanyi that's the female Uche because I am the male Uche. His other children include Emmanuel, Difu and Okechukwu. Francis Anyaeji had a relation Sir B.M Okorie who is the father of my good friends Kelechi and Chidinma Okorie. It was a large friendship with brother Obi doing his photography until he relocated to the US but later died. Sir B.M residence is at Number 66 Agunze road which is also my second home. His wife is Ogbuefi Rose Okorie who usually made us laugh. Sir B.M Okorie and Mr. Francis Anyaeji convinces me more that God would have created man in his own image and likeness. They were exceptional good men by every standard. The neighbourhood was fine and we had the Agorua family of Umuenu village living next to us at Number 9 Eneke Road. There was Emma, Nwafor, Ngozi, Arthur, Iyke, Ekene, Nkechi, Chukwuma and Collins all of the Agorua family. We had fun playing football in the neighbourhood and Mr. Christopher Agorua, the wife Ethel and Arthurs's mum (Mr. Agorua's second wife) were in a habit of telling us good old stories and opposite their house was that of Mr. George Ossai and Chioma Nzimiro the daughter of Professor Ikenna Nzimiro who lived in that house 11 Eneke road has been very close to my sister Ngozi. Roseline worked at the Health Office in Egwe on daily basis and they also made referral to the General Hospital Oguta which was well equipped and had medical experts in different fields of medicine. I recall Drs Izuagba, Ukoha, Nwoke and two others I cannot remember off heart.

Between 1988-1990, Roseline returned to the School of Health Technology Aba for a Diploma programme in Community Health Supervisor. From 1990-1997, Roseline continued to carry on with her duties as a nurse until her retirement. Roseline was not only a nurse but was also a Health administrator especially in the area of drug administration. At retirement, the attitude of the government towards Roseline and other retirees would almost lure me to ask if hard work actually pays?

As of April 2018, the government she served refused to pay pension for 11 months in 2015, 9 months in 2017 and 4 months in 2018.[65] The

---

[65] JOFAM Files, Nigeria Union of Pensioners "Arrears of Pension Owned by Imo State Government, 16-04-18

reward system in Nigeria is politely annoying and possesses every character obtainable in a failed state. Roseline was retired but not tired. Upon her husband's demise and retirement, she moved to Lagos in 1999 and in 2001 returned to Ndoro Umuahia to work in a private hospital. Her interest in training her children at the University paid off and she continued to work until 2004 when she decided to relocate home. The beautiful story is that Uche and Ngozi, her two children, had just graduated from the University.

Soucre: JOFAM Files.,Roseline Okonkwo with his son Uche during his Undergraduate Matriculation Ceremony in 1997

Source: JOFAM Files Uche Uwaezuoke Okonkwo graduates from University, 2000 set

FAMILY LIFE

In a marriage (both traditional and church marriage) consummated in 1978 respectively, Roseline got married to late Jeremaih Nnanna Okonkwo. The marriage of these two adults was well received. This is because Juliana Anyiwo the first daughter of Mrs. Agnes Okonkwo was married to an Isuikwuato man known as Julius Isilogwo Ndubuisi (also known as Uju nwere ego) of Umuebere aja village, Isuikwuato. Hence,

Isuikwuato was already well known route for the Okonkwo family.

Source: JOFAM FILES, Roseline I. Okonkwo dressing for her white wedding with Mrs Angelina Umeh (Her Sister in law), her chief bridesmaid and her friend Cecilia

Source: JOFAM FILES, Solemnization of marriage between Jerry Okonkwo & Roseline I. Okonkwo

Source: JOFAM FILES, Roseline I. Okonkwo with her Chief Bridesmaid arriving in a Renault Car of his brother Omenka

The union was blessed with two children namely Uche Uwaezuoke Okonkwo and Ngozi Ekine (nee Okonkwo). Uche studied History/ International Studies and holds a BA, MA, PGDE and PhD degrees specializing in Social and Imperial History of Africa. Uche won University of Lagos Graduate Fellowship from 2007-2009 for his PhD and has taught in Ebonyi State University Abakaliki, Federal University Wukari, Godfrey Okoye University and K.O Mbadiwe University. He was a Visiting Scholar at the Becker Freidman Institute, University of Chicago, USA and Scholar in resident at Harris School of Public Policy in the same institution from February to June, 2024. Uche had received travel grants and fellowships from esteemed organizations such as the United Nations Environment Programme, Spencer Foundation, Volvo Foundation, University of Bayeruth African Multiple Cluster, the Dutch Foundation for the History of Technology, and the Society for the History of Technology in Africa (SHOT). He had presented paper in universities across Africa, USA, Europe and Asia with over 100 conference papers and 100 articles in books and journals to his credit.

Source: JOFAM Files Uche Okonkwo& Ngozi Okonkwo as University Undergraduates in 1999.

Ngozi Ucheime Ekine (Nee Okonkwo) is a happily married to Hon Ignatius Ekine of Umutogwuma village Oguta. She graduated with B.Sc. degree in Banking and Finance from the Imo State University Owerri, Nigeria. She pursued postgraduate program and currently a carrier civil servant, wife and entrepreneur. She is the mother of two kids Ella and Ebunma.

Source: JOFAM Files, Emmanuella & Ebuma Ekine

Source: JOFAM Files, Roseline and her grandchild Kelechi Okonkwo

My encounters with Roseline as my mother are worth reflecting on here. The first was the promise she made to me as an infant to buy the 1940s brand of Volkswagen Beetle as soon as I secured admission to study medicine at the University. I opted for the arts and studied History up to the PhD level. I had expected a Volkswagen Beetle as mummy promised. She was quick to remind me that a PhD (Doctor of Philosophy) is not a Bachelor of Medicine and Surgery (MBBS). Our refusal (Uche & Ngozi) to study medical-related courses could be one way we couldn't fulfill her dreams perhaps.

At the All Saints Secondary School Aba in 1990, I had two sandals bought for me by mum.

One was made by Bata shoes and the other was a rubber sandal. I did not see the need for a rubber sandal since my classmates nicknamed it 'I fear no water'. One day it rained, I wore the sandal to school and it was my turn to laugh at those who wore leather sandals to school.

Roseline was firm and cherished her family a lot. However, she had a polite way of instilling discipline. I had insisted as a pupil of Ejemekwuru Community Primary School to fight a girl who had just visited us with the mother to Ejemekwuru in 1985. All efforts to make me not to fight the girl in question by my mother proved abortive. When the fight eventually commenced, the girl from Isuikwuato lifted me up and threw me on the floor. I shouted mummy *Ogu siri ike oo-* which means fight is difficult. She kept deaf ears to my plea of separating the fight. It was the only rare case my mum did not show concern to my plight. However, she warned me from onset not to fight the strong Isuikwuato girl. My dilemma refutes the Igbo popular saying that *nwoke luchaa ogu nwanyi enwere akuko* (when a man is done fighting, the woman tells the story). In my case, It was *nwanyi luchaa ogu nwoke enwere akuko* (when a woman is done fighting, the man tells the story).

In 1986, we went for a holiday in Isuikwuato. A crusade was organized by Rev. Fr. Emmanuel Edeh.

Everyone at home attended the crusade at Oguduasa, Isuikwuato. Edeh was a well-known Christian Charismatic figure of the 1980s. The clergy requested that those who do not love their mother should raise their hand. I was about to raise my hand when my mum brought my hand down. At home, she inquired why I was raising my hand at the crusade ground and I reminded her about her refusal to separate my fight with the Isuikwuato girl who got me beaten up. I insisted that I needed balls to play football as a way to make up for her negligence. She ordered two balls from the market in Akara, Isuikwuato and I enjoyed playing with a few folks in the village. I left one ball in Isuikwuato but returned with one to Ejemekwuru. This was how we reconciled our differences. My mother believed in me.

Roseline was a giver and sacrificed her income and time raising her two children. I recall on several occasions we had financial difficulties in school. She went borrowing to ensure we were taken care of. Regrettably, she never on such occasions tampered with public funds entrusted in her care to solve family problems. Even if she had to settle our urgent demands she would have been sure of her next income. However, church funds were a no-go area no matter the circumstance. Her irregular pension was spent on family issues and on few occasions, she usually issued authorization letters to enable Uche his son to visit the government sub-treasury to withdraw such money.

Source: JOFAM Files Roseline Okonkwo with Ngozi during her traditional marriages in 2010

Source: JOFAM Files Ngozi and Hon. Ignatius Ekine traditional marriages in 2010

Source: JOFAM Files, Roseline Okonkwo with infant Uche Uwaezuoke Okonkwo

Roseline's husband Jeremaih Okechukwu Okonkwo was formerly a soldier enlisted in Zaria in 1964/1965. By 1967, the secessionist attempt by the defunct Biafra led by Col. Ojukwu, left Jeremiah with the option of returning to Enugu to defend the new republic. As an experienced soldier, he fought with other patriots until 12 January 1970 when the war was formally declared over. Jerry had considered not returning back to the Nigerian army as an option. It was while trying to find his feet again that he met Roseline in the Effium and Ntezi axis of Abakaliki Division.

Bob as my mother refers to my father, will not let this young nurse to rest. Despite his relocation to Lagos in 1973, she kept in touch with Roseline until the marriage was consummated in 1978.

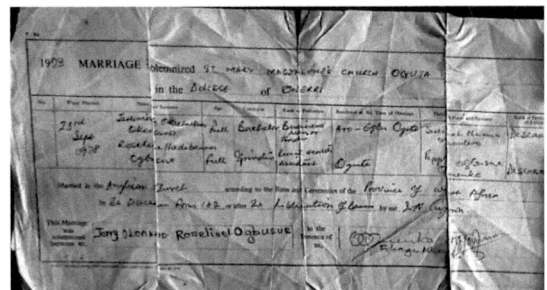

Source: JOFAM Files, Marriage Certificate between Roseline and Jeremaih Okonkwo

Source: JOFAM Files Jerry Okonkwo at the left and far right is his elder brother Godfrey Onuoha Okonkwo

Source: JOFAM Files. The photograph young Roseline Okonkwo with a friend

Source: JOFAM Files Jerry Okonkwo at the left and far right is his friend Bestman Nwankwo

The posting of Rose to Oguta especially the creation of Imo State in 1976 was not difficult for the government. Coincidentally, the elder brother Rev Omenka was also posted to Trinity High School Oguta. Omenka as I mentioned early was known in Oguta in the late 1970's and 1980's for his dedication to duty. Hardly could anyone have studied in Oguta during this period without drinking from Omenka's fountain of knowledge. Many people in Oguta today who became successful academics, intellectuals, businessmen, career civil servants and teachers could easily recall Omenka each time the name is mentioned. This speaks in volume of the defining character and dedication to duty of the Roseline family people.

Source: JOFAM Files. The photograph was Uche Okonkwo's 1 year birthday with other members of the family Ogechi Omenka, Chima Umeh, Uwaoma Omenka and others

Roseline's choice of marriage to Jeremiah of Egbuoma village in Oguta was built on her selflessness and humility. Egbuoma as a town appeared in academic records only in 1854 when an European ethnographer W.B Baikie in his book *Narrative of An Exploring Voyage Up the Rivers Kwora and Binue commonly known as the Niger and Tsadda* wrote about the place as follows: "After the Abo territory proper commences, the first town in it being Ase. Opposite the south end of Bullocks Island, to the eastward, is the district of Obagwe (meaning Obeagwa people the first settlers in Oguta) with a time of the same name, below which is Ugidi (Ugada), which is situated in Akra-Ugidi (Akara Ugada). To the southward of Ugidi (Ugada), still near the river at Ogu (Ogwu) and further down the district and town of Egboma (meaning Egbuoma). Rather behind Egboma (Egbuoma) stands Uguta (meaning Oguta), the inhabitants which come to the river for fishing and trading".[47]

This author examined the Abo territory and the settlement of Egbuoma and Oguta people over time. By 1889, A.F Mockler Ferryman had written about Oguta after his visit to the town.[66] John Goodchild account of Igbo Bible translation (1905-

---

[66]   Uche Uwaezuoke Okonkwo, 'Women in Pre-colonial Igbo Society: A Case of Oguta, *MA thesis in History,* University of Lagos, 2006,16

1913) led by the Church Missionary Society (CMS sheds light about Egbu (not Egbu Owerri). Records has it that Mr. Onyeabo one of the Bible translators led by Archdeacon Dennis had friends in Egbu Oguta that usually welcomes the missionaries.[67] On 18 May 1905, Archdeacon Dennis and his group slept in the house of Akenkwo (Anyiwo) in Umueze-awala (most likely Umuezeala) whom he described as Umucuku (Umuchukwu man) known to his friends in Egbu.[68] The Umuchukwu had over time lived in many places in Egbu until the finally settled in their present location. Elsewhere, I have written that Umuchukwu people lived in Ubaramehi precisely in Amaubilaso.[69] Around 16 August 1910 on arrival to Egbu, Archdeacon Dennis saw a lad living with Rev A.C Onyeabo and Rev. Payne trying to preach to his people.[70] This lad was later catechist George Ijeoma Okereke Anyiwo.

The Anyiwo family is the birth place of two sisters namely Ucheime Anyiwo (later married to the Nwokoye family in Obosi) and Agnes Anyiwo (later married to the Okonkwo family). Agnes

[67] John Goodchild, *Dennis and the Ibo Bible*, Norwich, JohnGood Child,2003, 144

[68] Goodchild, *Dennis and the Ibo Bible*,147

[69] Uche Uwaezuoke Okonkwo, *They Were Not the Last to Settle in the Land: A History of Aro Network in Oguta Axis*, Nsukka, University of Nigeria Press, 2018,32

[70] Goodchild, *Dennis and the Ibo Bible*,227

marriage to late Nnanna Jeremaih Okonkwo in late 1930's gave birth to Godfrey Onuoha Okonkwo, Angelina Ekwutosi Okonkwo and Jeremaih Okechukwu Okonkwo who was Roseline's husband (1978-1998). Before her marriage to Nnanna Jeremiah Okonkwo, Agnes had Juliana Anyiwo who later got married in Isuikwuato. The road to Isuikwuato had since always been symbiotic relationship in the family tradition.

Mama Agnes husband Pa Nnanna Okonkwo died in 1949 and had other siblings like Okwuobasi Paul Okonkwo, Micheal Okonkwo and three sisters Jemaimah Mgborie Anyiwo (nee Okonkwo), Ugwuezi Ogbonna (nee Okonkwo) and Priscilla Anyiwo which has been captured in the family chart below.

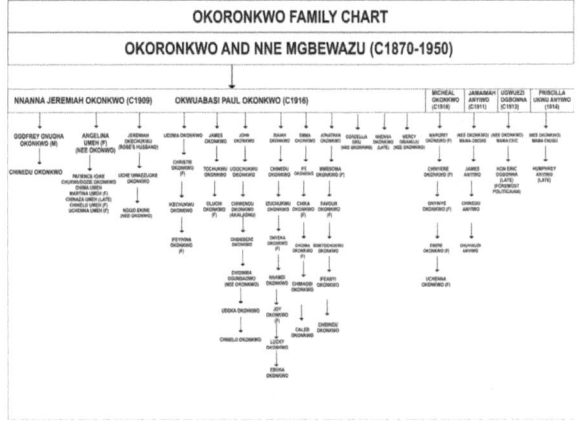

The above account provides an excellent historical tradition associated with Roseline's place of marriage. Onyeka Onwenu had described Agnes (Roseline's mother in-law) in the following way:

> Mama Nnukwu had a sister whom we call Mama Obele, which translates to Small Mama. Her proper name was Agnes Okonkwo. Perhaps this may explain why Mama Nnukwu was so enamored by my song 'Nwa Aginesi. This sisters were friends and business partners; together They undertook the supply of food items to Aggrey Memorial College. Mama lived in Abakaliki where they Sourced items such as rice, beans, garri and dry fish popularly known as azu mangala, which were supplied back to the school. It was a grueling journey they made from Obosi to Abakaliki, and then Arochukwu huddled in the passenger seats of the lorry, enduring all of its discomforts. The roads to these remote places were not the

best, but these two women bore their troubles with dignity and pride. They also made very good money.[71]

Source: JOFAM Files, Mrs Agnes Okonkwo (Roseline's Mother in-law)

---

[71]   Onyeka Onwenu, *My Father's Daughter*, Lagos, Expand Press Ltd, 2020, 54-55

The relationship between Agnes and Ucheime is still sustained till date. Ucheime's children Ernest Nwokoye, Hope Onwenu and Dorathy Ejindu as cousins with Roseline's husband Jeremaih were always showing interest in our growth. The children of Hope Onwenu namely Prof. Ijeoma Otigbue, Chukwudum Onwenu, Prof. Dibugwu Onwenu and Onyeka Onwenu are Jeremaih Okonkwo's second cousins. Hope Onwenu lived with Jeremaih Okonkwo in the same building in Ikate Surulere Lagos for almost two decades. Onyeka Onwenu my father's best friend and cousin was so close to us that she had mentioned Uche and Ngozi in her 1980's lyrics titled *Onye ga agba egwu.*

Source: JOFAM Files, Uche Okonkwo second year birthday with Onyenaturuchi Adimonyema, Chima Umeh, Aunty Olivia and others

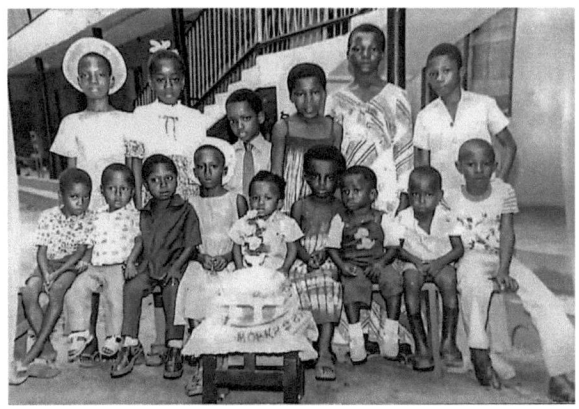

Source: JOFAM Files, Uche okonkwo at three attending a birthday accompanied by Grace Okorie and Chima Umeh

Agnes had made good old money from trade and once owned a building in Effium in Abakaliki Division. It was Roseline's sincerity and sense of duty that attracted her to Mama Agnes love and of course the marriage between her and Jerry which lasted between 1978-1998. Mama Agnes had clout and did not usually give up in the pursuit of fortunes. She was instrumental to the marriage of his brother-in-law Okwuobasi's marriage to Mama Ola. Agnes died in 1991 at the age of 85. There are other women of Abakaliki area married to the Okoronkwo/Uchenivu extended kindred most probably because of Agnes recommendations.

CHAPTER FOUR

SERVICE TO THE CHURCH, HEALTH CHALLENGES AND DEATH

Upon her return to Egbuoma in 2004 for her final retirement, she was devoted to the things of God as well as St. Mary's Anglican Church Egbuoma which was founded in 1912. Her contribution to the church was summarized by Rev Sydney Arize who had served in the church and wrote thus:

> Mama Rose was a very dedicated, committed, faithful and honest communicant. A lover of both God and things of God. Till I was posted out from St Mary Anglican Church Egbuoma in June 2019, Mama Rose did not absent from morning prayers, Friday class and victory hour despite her age. Her level of

faith and Commitment challenged me. She never gets discouraged no matter the circumstances or challenge. A generous giver and lover of God's servant has gone home to be with his maker.[72]

Her uncommon faith in Christendom especially the Evangelic Fellowship in Anglican Communion (EFAC) was exemplary. She was committed to the growth of the Mother's Union (MU) and was regularly engaged in programmes that took her to other parishes. She made cleaning the Church her hubby and believed strongly that if you work for God he will not forsake you. In recognition of her selfless service, she was honoured in 2015 as the daughter of Zion.

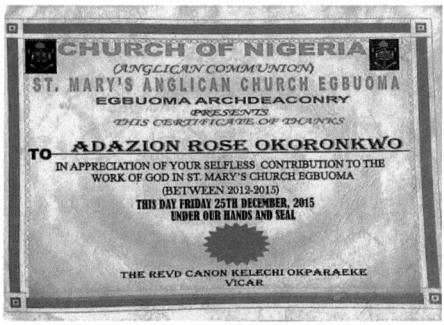

---

[72]   Rev. Sydney Arize post on Okonkwo Uche 79 Facebook Wall, accessed 16 November 2024

She was at a time responsible for church finances and accountability was her watch word. Her devotion to duty was exemplified in so many ways she was prudent and diligent in managing church affairs. Her sense of hard work is still a reference point.

Source: JOFAM Files, Roseline and other Christian mothers at St Mary's Anglican Church Egbuoma

Around 2017, signs of aging were beginning to set in, especially incessant back and leg pains. Yet with courage, she moved on and saw it as a distraction to draw her back from the things of God. This was the development until August 2024. Rose was beginning to show signs of weakness and was unable to keep fit and agile as she used to be. She was moved to her daughter's place in Owerri but yet hopeful she was that this phase was just another trial time.

On Sunday 27 October 2024, it was the last time she lived on earth. She has gone to the hospital complaining of an increased heartbeat. All efforts by the medical team at the specialist hospital proved abortive. She requested to lie down while on life support and was doing everything she could to stay. When she was convinced it was the end she muttered 'the end has come, life is vanity".

CHAPTER FIVE

EPILOGUE

This is a concise biography of a very private woman and a nurse from Eluama Isuikwuato. I have in this monograph provided an account of the genealogical history of two Igbo families the Omenka and Okonkwo. Roseline Okonkwo is actually the focus but I made bold attempt to connect how human interactions over time have aided family growth and survival.

Enriched in strong historical traditions, I have argued about the Eurocentric misrepresentation of facts by the colonial intelligence report of 1933 by the District Officer in charge of Okigwe. I attempted an account of the origin of the people and traced the family background of Roseline. I insisted on creating a gap to be covered by upcoming historians.

The educational system offered to Rose was examined, especially the plight of the Girl Child (GC) in pursuit of Western education. Applying a multiplicity of sources, I made a case on how Roseline rose above the barriers created by cultural restrictions. As an extension of Eurocentric Victorianism, women of the Roseline era during the colonial period were to be seen but not heard. Above these restrictions, she excelled through a stint of hard work.

She secured a job in 1962 and stayed on duty until the outbreak of the Nigerian Civil War in 1967. The War which ended in 1970 was examined in this monograph as unnecessary and a major setback to the progress of Igbo people in Nigeria. My conviction is that the war was a class struggle by the elites in the army who were blinded by ethnic dreams instead of national cohesion. Col. Ojukwu's declaration of war with less than 500 mundane guns and arming youths with cutlasses and knives is considered in this monograph as the worst leadership deceit in human history.

Roseline survived the war but the scars of war resurfaced with the rise of Unknown Gun (UG) and pro-Biafran agitations which have been ubiquitous in Orlu zone not excluding Egbuoma where Roseline lived. The psychological trauma of military invasions into respective Igbo towns is unhealthy and the history of memories may suffer fallibility in trying to capture the exactitude of the events that took place between the federal troops and organized resistance and neo-Biafranism from 2021-2024.

I discussed Roseline's family life and provided an account of her struggle to survive upon her husband's death in 1998 when Uche the son was in the second year of the University and Ngozi was about to secure University admission. Her retirement with neglected benefits most time unpaid for affected the family in a multiplicity of ways. I outlined and discussed her approaches to life, commitment to duty, and sincerity.

Roseline died in October 2024 but had lived a life of hard work, struggle, honesty, and humility. A few tributes poured in upon her demise and have been incorporated as part of the Focus Group Discussion (FGD) in this book.

BIBLIOGRAPHY

NATIONAL ARCHIVES ENUGU

NAE (Hereafter National Archives Enugu), CSE 1/85/4132, File No EP 7576 A, Intelligence Report on Isu Ikwu Ato clan by Mr V.Fox Strangeways, District Officer Okigwe, 1930-1933

NAE, OKDIST 4/14/28, A Letter from Chief Ejeafor of Amibo to the Worship District Officer Okigwe, 27 August 1932

NAE, OKDIST 4/14/28, A Letter from Ujombu Akamadu to the District Office Okigwi, 14 June 1932

NAE, OKDIST 6/1/54, A Letter from the Central Office Native Administration to the Native Authority Isuikwuato 'Nonya-Eluama Road' 15 June 1953

NAE, OKDIST 9/1/106, Elders and Ezealas of Isuikwuato: Petition From

NAE, OKDIST 9/1/109, A Memo from ETC Ennals the Assistant District Officer Okigwi 'Report on Council Reorganization in Isuikwuato Clan

NAE, OKDIST 9/1/159, A Letter from the District Officer Okigwe to the Resident Owerri Province Portharcourt Ísuikwuato Clan' 27 October 1938

NAE, OKDIST 9/1/159, Report on Council Re-Organization in Isuikwuato Clan

NAE, OKDIST 9/1/241B, Isuikwuato Clan Tax

NAE, OKDIST 9/1/241B, Proposals for the Future Administartive and Judicial Organization of Isu-ikwu-Ato Clan

NAE, OKDIST 9/1/126, A Memorandum from the District Officer Okigwe Division to the Resident Owerri Province Portharcourt, 10 October 1936

NAE, OKDIST 9/1/126, A Memorandum from the District Officer Okigwe Division to the Resident Owerri Province Portharcourt 'Ebi and Others, 10 October 1936

NAE, OKDIST 9/1/126, A Memorandum from the District Officer Okigwe Division to the Resident Owerri Province Portharcourt 'Ebi and Others, 26 January 1937

JEREMAIH OKONKWO FAMILY ARCHIVES & MUSEUM (JOFAM)

JOFAM Files, Income Tax P.A.Y.E Receipt, 1976-1997

JOFAM Files, Mgborokwu D.M ''Salary Progression in Respect of Mrs R.I Okonkwo

JOFAM Files, Nigeria Union of Pensioners ''Arrears of Pension Owned by Imo State Government, 16-04-18

JOFAM Files, Records of Service (Cond) Africansta

UNPUBLISHED THESES/MATERIALS

Burial Programme of Rev. Omenka O. Omenka at Wesley Methodist Church Cathedral,Eluama, Isuikwuato, 28-07-2018

Eke-Aghukwa, Ihuoma Ngozi A Historical Survey of Ahaa (Ahaba) in Isuikwuato Local Government Area Before the 1900, *BA Project in History*, June 1983

Ekekwe James Obinna, A History of the Apostolic Faith Church of Jesus Christ in Amaba Isuikwuato (1941-1960), *B.A Project in History and International Studies,* University of Nigeria, October, 2007

Mbonye, Francis Onyebuchi, 'External Trade of Isuikwuato in the Nineteenth Century" *BA Project, Department of History,* University of Nigeria, Nsukka, June 1987

Ndukwe, L.O, Isuikwuato: "A Pre Colonial Economy" *BA Project, Department of History, University of Nigeria, Nsukka, April,* 1995

Nwankwo, Chinyere I, 'International Organizations and the Development of Primary Health care in Nigeria, 1988-2009, *BA Project, Department of History, UNN* April, 2009

Nwosu Joseph Ihedinihu, The Nigerian Civil War and Isuikwuato Women, *BA Project in History, University of Nigeria, Nsukka*, April 1995

Ogbuagu Adibe Chukwuma, "Warfare in Pre-olonial Isuikwuato" *BA Project Department of History,* University of Nigeria,Nsukka, June, 1989

Okonkwo, U.U, 'Women in Pre-colonial Igbo Society: A Case of Oguta, *MA thesis in History,* University of Lagos, 2006

Okoronkwo O. Kingdom, Christianity and Western Education in Isuikwuato 1906-1994, *BA Project,* of Nigeria, Nsukka, 1981

Onyenkpa, Chijioke Onyebuchi"A Historical Survey of Isuikwuato Before 1900: Origins, Pattern of Migration and Settlement and

Political Organization", *BA Project History and Archaeology*, University of Nigeria, Nsukka, 1981

Umejiaku Vera Uche, 'Local Government and Community Development in Isuikwuato LGA 1976-2000, *BA Project History and International Studies,* University of Nigeria, Nsukka, 2019

BOOKS/ JOURNALS

Achebe, C, Home *and Exile*, London, Penguin Publishing Group, 2001

Afigbo, A., *Ropes of Sand: Studies in Igbo History and Culture*, Ibadan, University Press Ltd, 1981

Adiele. E. Afigbo, "The Native Treasury Question under the Warrant Chief System in Eastern Nigeria 1899-1929", *Odu: University of Ife Journal of African Studies* 4, no.1, (1967): 30-32.

Ajayi, Simon. Ademola, Who is Not Afraid of History? Inaugural Lecture 2021/2022, University of Ibadan, Friday 6 July 2023

Akoda, W.E *From the Abyss of Memory: Efiong Ukpong Aye, Calabar*, Desertwater Communications, 2011

Alakwe, V.A, *The History of Nkwerre-Isu Igbo*, Glasboro, Goldline and Jacobs Publishing, 2020, *As the Niger and Tsadda in 1854, London*, Frankcass and Co. Ltd, 1960

Awasom, Nicodemus Fru & Bojang, Ousman M, 'Bifurcated World of African Nationalist Historiography" *Lagos Historical Review Vol.9*, 2009

Baikie,W.B, *The Narrative of An Exploring Voyage Up the Rivers Kwora and Binue Commonly Known* London, Frank Cass and Co Ltd, 1966

Chijioke Ngobili, Ugwu Nwasike: The Man, The Name, The Monument: The Authored Biography of Warrant Chief Timothy Muodozie Nwasike of Ikenga-Ogidi 1879-1970, Lagos, Hillysyke Foundations, 2022

Goodchild, J, *Dennis and the Ibo Bible*, Norwich, JohnGood Child, 2003

Hubbard, L, The Night Nurses, *Callalo*, Vol.39, No.4, 2016

Imbua, D.L 'Robbing Others to Pay Mary Slessor: Unearthing the Authentic Heroes and Heroines of the Abolition of Twin-Killing in Calabar, African *Economic History, Vol.41, 2013*

Isichei, E, Igbo *Worlds: An Anthology of Oral Histories and Historical Descriptions* London and, Basingstoke, Macmillan, 1977

Mba, Nina E, *Ayoji Rosiji Man With Vision*, Ibadan, Spectrum Books, 1992

Murphy, Beatrice Diary of A Night Nurse, Butte, Montana, 1909, *Montana The Magazine of Western of Western History, Vol.39 No.4, Autumn 1989*

Nwankwo, A.A, Nigeria: The Challenge of Biafra, Enugu, Fourth Dimension, 1972

Okonkwo and Chijioke Chinoyerem Ekebuisi ed. *A Centenary of Archdeacon Dennis Union Igbo*, Uturu, Gregory University Press, 2018

Okonkwo, U.U, 'Archdeacon Dennis Union Igbo Through the Prisms of History" in Uche Uwaezuoke Okonkwo, U.U, They Were Not the Last to Settle in the Land: A History of Aro Network in Oguta Axis, Nsukka, University of Nigeria Press, 2018

Onwenu, Onyeka *My Father's Daughter*, Lagos, Expand Press Ltd, 2020

Phyllis Johnson, Eye of Fire Emeka Anyaoku, Ibadan, Spectrum Books, 2000

Udeagha, Mazi C.O, 'Trade and Trade Routes Within The Okigwe Area in the 19th Century" *TransAfrican Journal of History, Vol.16, 1987*

INTERNET AND SOCIAL MEDIA SOURCES

History and Foundation-Nursing Fundamentals-pressbooks.pub, http://wtcs.pressbooks.pub accessed 2 November 2024

Isuikwuato Local Government Area of Nigeria, http://www.citypopulation accessed 12 November, 2024

Rev. Sydney Arize post on Okonkwo Uche 79 Facebook Wall, accessed 16 November 2024

Top 3 Nurses in Nigerian History Who Made Significant Changes, http:// dailytimesng.com accessed 3 November 2024

Yolanda Smith, History of Nursing, http://news-medical.net accessed 16 October 2024

APPENDIX/TRIBUTES

FOREVER IN MY HEART

Mummy, the pain of losing you is so great that words cannot adequately express it. I am yet to come to terms with the brutal fact that you are no more.

I was 18 years old when we lost our dad, you played the role of both mother and father. All through our challenging times, you were resilient and trusted in God. You never gave up. You sacrificed your very last and comfort to see us through our academic pursuit. You were a virtuous woman and my role model.

My super mum, a mum like no other, Ada Zion, an epitome of love, peace, and kindness, is a woman with a golden heart. How could the cold breeze of death come and snatch you away? I watched while you passed on, a memory that will always be fresh in my heart you will forever be missed in my life. You lived a life to the Glory of God and had strong faith in God. I pray to God to help me live above your good conduct so that my children will see me as their role model and with a good testament of me in the sand of time.

May the gate of heaven welcome your gentle soul. Rest on my dear mum till we meet again.

Your Daughter,
Mrs Ngozi Ekine

TRIBUTE TO MY GRANDMOTHER

It is with a heavy heart that I write this. Though your time was up, it was still shocking the way you left. On that day you left for the hospital, I thought you would come back like always. I expected your arrival but never saw you again. The news of your death was really sad and surprising. Though I came into your life 15 years ago, I can firmly say my GrandMa was a peaceful, hardworking, considerate, and God-fearing woman whom I will forever look up to.

Though you may be gone, your sweet memories will forever live in our hearts. I will forever miss you but I know everything happens for a reason. I bid you farewell Grand Ma and may your gentle soul keep on resting in peace. Amen

Your Grandchild,
Ella

TRIBUTE TO MY GRANDMOTHER

Grandma, I was shocked when Mummy told me you are no more. When you came to stay with us, I was very happy. I never knew death would take you away from us. I remember those times we would come to visit and the way you pampered us. Your absence will be tough for us to bear. You were kind and peaceful. I believe you are in heaven Grand Ma. We are missing you, grandma.

May your soul rest in peace

Your grandchild,
Ebunma

TRIBUTE TO MY MOTHER IN LAW

I feel heavily laden with grief over your demise. During your lifetime, you showed love to people around you. Through your hard work, faithfulness, and fidelity, you built a wonderful family to the glory of God.

At the beginning of creation, God made man and woman to form a family unit. I remember vividly the first day I came to intimate you of my desire to marry your daughter, you welcomed me with open arms. You accepted me wholeheartedly and you were not materialistic.

You were extremely a wonderful mother, patient and understanding, an example to all the women in her generation. You had a heart of gold, always seeking the positive side in everybody.

Adieu, my good mother-in-law till we meet again, and may your gentle soul rest in the bosom of the lord.

Your Son-in-law,
Hon Ekine Ignatius

TRIBUTE TO NMA UCHE, NMA NGOZI OKONKWO

Nma Uche! I and my wife planned to visit you towards the end of this year with our children. A few days before death struck, my mum asked if the Oguta trip would still be this year. I affirmed the fact that the plans for the trip have not changed. Munachi and Chizaram kept asking Daddy when are we going to Oguta to see Nma Uche? Honestly, I am pained that I could not visit you this year.

The last we spoke on the phone, you asked after my mum, Nma Ndy, Nma Uchechi, Bro Nwosu, and Sunny. Nma Uche you are so kind. So gentle, so warm to everyone. You took care of us in Oguta. You also did the same in Aba.

Nma Uche your existence was too soon for me and my siblings. Words cannot describe the loss we feel. We will always treasure you. May your soul rest in peace Nma Uche, Mama Ngozi, and Sister Nwanne. Amen

From,

Hon. Omenka O. Omenka, Uwaoma Omenka, Amarachukwu Omenka and Ngozi Omenka

A TRIBUTE TO MY BELOVED SISTER IN LAW MRS ROSELINE IHEDIWANMA OKONKWO ALIAS NWANE

Today we gather to honour the life of a remarkable humble and virtuous woman Sister Rose Ihediwanma fondly called Nwane. Sister Nwane was a beacon of love and her name depicts it. Jesus is referred to as the Rose of Sharon in the Songs of Solomon 2 Vs 1.

The fragrance of Jesus, the Rose of Sharon was her identity. She had him in her life blooming and glowing. The sweet smell of the presence of God was always around us. She was full of milk of human kindness. She had no axe to grind with anybody. She was a lady seen and not heard but full of wisdom, knowledge, and strength. A rare gem. God endured her with a heart of gold, gentle, unassuming, and peaceful. These qualities made her live in peace with everybody. Nwane touched many lives, some are here today to mourn her departure. To God be the glory.

Sister Nwane and her late sister Mrs Comfort Oduagu Umahi showered us with love. The love they had for their only brother was extended to me and my children. We have very sweet memories of them. Sister Nwane your departure was a shock to us. We did not hear that you were sick only to be told that you have gone to meet your maker. Your transition is painful because we will not see you again physically. Your sweet memories live in our hearts. We cannot question God the author and finisher of our faith but we are consoled by the fact that you ran a good race and lived a righteous life, impacted positively to your family. Your paternal family and the entire people of Umuihe Umuama Eluama Isuikwuato.

The Rose, may your gentle soul rest in peace. We loved you but God loved you most. Rest in the bosom of the Almighty till the resurrection morning when we shall part no more. Adieu Mama Uche, Mama Ngozi, Nwunye Bob, Ulu Pepple Omenka and Nwane nne ya Keziah Omenka.

Your Sister-in-law,
Elder Mrs. Bridget Omenka

TRIBUTE TO MY DEAR AUNTIE MRS ROSELINE I. OKOKWO(NEE OMENKA)

Words will certainly not be enough to express how heartbroken I was when the news of your demise reached me. At the next in the line of birth(immediate) younger sister to my late mother 'Umahi Comfort Oduagu',. Your love and care to both myself and my late brother 'Obineche' was so glaring that we were always holidaying with you, visiting you at all the stations you were posted as a Nurse.

You were unconditionally accommodating. In matters of discipline, Auntie was routinely fair, firm and uncompromising. To us under your care, we must do our house chore timely,observe our afternoon siesta, eat at the appropriate time; above all we all learnt to commune with God early mornings and evenings before retiring to bed.

On medical attention to us and my larger family (a profession she loves so much), my auntie was always there for us. Today, we mourn. Today we celebrate. We mourn the our dear auntie and we also at once celebrate her life; a life near perfection and well lived. To Uche, Ngo and families weep no more for God has won and will always win. It is the way of all mortals. May her lovely and gentle soul rest in peace.

Adieu my Auntie.

Elder,
Engr. Umahi Henry Chukwunenye and Family